10664782

Reverse the Curse
In Your Body
And Emotions

Annette Capps

ANNETTE CAPPS MINISTRIES
P.O. Box 10
Broken Arrow, OK 74013
U.S.A.

Unless otherwise indicated,
all scriptural quotations are taken from
the *King James Version* of the Bible.

11th Printing 2014
66,500 in print

Reverse the Curse
ISBN 13: 978-0-9618975-0-5
ISBN 10: 0-9618975-0-3
Copyright © 1987 by Annette Capps Ministries
P.O. Box 10
Broken Arrow, OK 74013
U.S.A.

Published by
Capps Publishing
PO Box 69
England, AR 72046

Contents

Foreword

One of the most needed teachings in the Church today is in the area of the emotions. Countless Christians are sick physically and emotionally because of a lack of knowledge about the mind. As I have taught these principles throughout the United States, I have seen many set free in their minds and then in their bodies.

After I began this teaching, I received tremendous response from people who wanted tapes and instruction concerning this area of life. If a person is emotionally bound, it is difficult for him to receive healing and stay healed. This is not a book on psychology, but a teaching from God's Word with practical instruction to help you live an abundant life in Jesus Christ.

Annette Capps

Chapter 1
Reverse the Curse in Your Emotions

What I teach concerning the emotions is not a theory I developed. I myself have struggled with the same emotions that many of you have. Fear of failure, rejection, inferiority, and depression were part of my life unitl the Holy Spirit taught me the principles in this book.

I knew that Christ had redeemed me from the curse of the law according to Galatians 3:13. I also knew the curse of the law included poverty, sickness, and death. What I did not realize was that part of that sickness was emotional and mental sickness. Most of you who are reading this book are not seriously mentally ill, but you are where I was: mentally and emotionally *bound*. Christ redeemed us from every kind of emotional and mental sickness.

The Lord shall smite thee with madness, and blindness, and aston-

1

ishment of heart:

And thou shalt grope at noonday, as the blind gropeth in darkness, and thou shalt not prosper in thy ways: and thou shalt be only oppressed and spoiled evermore, and no man shall save thee.

Thou shalt betroth a wife, and another man shall lie with her: thou shalt build an house, and thou shalt not dwell therein: thou shalt plant a vineyard, and shalt not gather the grapes thereof.

Thine ox shall be slain before thine eyes, and thou shalt not eat thereof: thine ass shall be violently taken away from before thy face, and shall not be restored to thee: thy sheep shall be given unto thine enemies, and thou shalt have none to rescue them.

Thy sons and thy daughters shall be given unto another people, and thine eyes shall look, and fail with longing for them all the day long: and there shall be no might in thine hand.

The fruit of thy land, and all thy labours, shall a nation which thou knowest not eat up; and thou shalt be only oppressed and crushed away:

So that thou shall be mad for the

sight of thine eyes which thou shalt see.

Deuteronomy 28:28-34

The first thing I want to point out to you is that the Hebrew says, *"The Lord will allow you to be smitten . . ."* God is *not* the author of sickness, whether mental or physical. When the children of Israel were disobedient, they stepped out of God's protection into the devil's territory. And when they did so, destruction overtook them.

The curse here was madness — insanity and oppression. Insanity and oppression begin with a thought which develops into an abnormal state of mind. When an individual becomes oppressed and then depressed in the mental realm, it often opens the door for demonic activity. Demons desire to take over the minds and the bodies of human beings. If Satan can begin by oppressing you with negative thoughts, then he can move further against you.

I am not speaking of demonic possession here. Christians can be oppressed (or troubled, pressed upon) by spirits of darkness, but not possessed. A negative thought develops into a thought pattern. A negative thought pattern alters a person's ability to relate positively to others. Then that individual will sense rejection. After rejection, depression comes. If the depression is not broken, a demonic spirit will attempt to prolong the depression and bring the person into total mental and emotional bondage.

We can reverse this curse by being obedient to God's Word and accepting what Jesus has done at Calvary. Through the Name of Jesus, bondage can be broken and demons dismissed. But it is our goal to remain free of the curse once that bondage has been broken.

Jesus Bore the Emotional Curse

Emotional healing was accomplished for us on Calvary, but we must appropriate and enforce it. To enforce it, we must act on God's Word and guard our minds from thoughts the enemy would place there.

Let us look into some Scriptures from the Word of God concerning the mind and emotions.

> **Beloved, I wish above all things that thou mayest prosper and be in health, even as thy soul prospereth.**
> **3 John 2**

Prospering in Your Soul

It is difficult to prosper in any area of

your life, whether it be in your physical body, your relationships, your finances, or any other realm, when you are not prospering in the soulish area. The soulish realm — your mind, your will and your emotions — is where the battleground is.

For many years I've heard sermons that dealt with physical healing, salvation, and other subjects in the Bible, but seldom have I heard any messages that dealt with the soul, the mind, and the emotions. It seems that Christians are afraid of the mental realm because of such things as Christian Science, the metaphysical, mind control, and other cults. But the Word of God teaches that we have authority over the soulish area of our life. Let us look at some Scriptures that deal with the soulish area.

> **He that hath no rule over his own spirit is like a city that is broken down, and without walls.**
> **Proverbs 25:28**
> **He that is slow to anger is better than the mighty; and he that ruleth his spirit than he that taketh a city.**
> **Proverbs 16:32**

Keep Your Walls Up

Isn't this an interesting comparison? The Word says, *"He that ruleth his spirit* [is better than] *he that taketh a city."* Contrasting that, the Word of God says, *"He that hath no rule over his own spirit is like a city that is broken down, and without walls."*

Imagine for a moment what cities looked like in the days of the Bible. Their greatest protection were the walls that encircled the city. At night the inhabitants shut the gates, guarded the walls, and watched for intruders. The walls were built to protect the city and its inhabitants. If enemies tried to get in, they had to go over the walls or come in through the gates. Of course, if they gained access into the city, they could spoil, ravage, and kill its inhabitants. So it was very important to keep the walls and gates in good repair.

This is a marvelous comparison to the spiritual, emotional, and mental condition of a man or a woman. If you don't guard your own spirit, your own heart, you are like a city whose walls are broken down — and you have no protection. You are then opened to all kinds of violence and destruction.

Many psychologists have insisted that we should not have these walls. "Don't put walls up; people with walls have problems," they have said. But we are talking about a different kind of wall. The walls we are discussing are built to keep aliens and intruders out — not to keep the inhabitants locked in. Nor do these walls prevent those who are no threat from entering.

Many people have the wrong walls built up. They have locked themselves inside a prison of fear. No one is allowed in for fear of hurt. Do you know what would happen to a city if it never opened its gates? The inhabitants would starve and die! Many people are in that emotional state. They are starving emotionally and spiritually because they have shut everyone out. We all need interaction with others. Some people must be allowed to enter the gates of our city; others must not.

God has not left our spirit or heart wide open to assault and hurt. He gave us a mind with the power of choice as a wall to protect our heart and emotions. Your spirit is like the inner city where the inhabitants live. That's where most of the activities of the city are carried on. We can compare this to Proverbs 4:23, which states that out of the heart *are the issues of life.* The most important activities take place in the heart or spirit, and it must be protected. Your mind contains the wall and gates that will guard your heart.

The point is that to be emotionally and

mentally healthy, we must not lock ourselves in, but we do have the power of
decision, the ability to choose *whom* and *what*
we let in! It is in your control if you rule your
own spirit!

Chapter 2
The Mind
Is the Battleground

Satan cannot directly attack your heart. He has to work from the outside in. Where does he begin? Obviously, with the mind and thoughts. He attacks from outside the walls, battling you with thoughts so you'll open the gate. Once he gets past the gate of your decision-making ability, your emotions are directly affected. What you feel (your emotions) is a direct result of the thoughts that you have accepted into your mind.

To prove the point, let's talk about anger. Have you ever become angry for no reason, without a thought first? Seriously, do you know anyone sitting on a comfortable sofa on a beautiful day in a wonderful mood who suddenly became violently angry with no provocation? (Except the seriously mentally ill.) Of course not! The emotion of anger is produced by a thought or perception of wrongdoing. We all have heard someone

9

say, "The more I *thought* about it, the madder I got!" You let your thoughts get out of control, and so did your emotions (anger). Your emotions always follow your thoughts. You lost the rule over your spirit, and in doing so developed some holes in your walls!

Diligence

What happened to this city to cause the walls to be broken down and the city ruined? First, the inhabitants of the city were not diligent. When the wall began to fall into disrepair, they did not check for holes or weaknesses that could have developed. Second, there were many battles going on, with direct attacks upon the city. As the enemy began to penetrate the city and assault the gates, much damage was done. Damage must be repaired, or it will accumulate.

Your spirit, your inner man, is like the inside of that city. The wall that is protecting that city is the soulish realm — your mind, your will, and your emotions. Any damage done to your mind and emotions must be repaired immediately so your walls will remain strong to protect you.

You must protect your heart. It is very important, and it requires much diligence on your part. You cannot throw yourself wide open for everything that comes along. I know people who are emotional basket cases. They have no control whatsoever over their emotions. Then there are people who don't seem to have *any* emotions, or at least they don't show any. Neither of these states is healthy. There is a balance we must strive for.

The walls become broken down, just as your emotions can become broken down, because of the attacks on your mind. That is where the devil attacks you first — in your mind. *Your mind is the battleground of satanic attack.* That is why you must diligently guard what goes into it.

Declare aloud:

I have a mind. It is the battleground where I win!

I do not accept defeat.

My mind belongs to me, not the devil.

Therefore, I can win!

Everyday you are dealing with your mind and Satan's attacks upon it. How many times has the devil ever told you that you were a failure? Has that thought ever come to your mind? He tells you:

"You are a failure."

"You are stupid."

"You never do anything right."

"You are ugly."

These suggestions are an attack upon your mind to destroy your inner man. If Satan can ruin your self-image and give you a "failure complex," he can wreck the rest of your life!

You must be diligent to guard against these attacks on your self-esteem. Learn to stop Satan's lies from entering your gates and becoming thought patterns in your life. It will take some time to learn this. But as you practice, you will enjoy great results. One person may have a tendency to procrastinate, while another has a tendency to feel sorry for himself and wallow in self-pity. Define your specific battleground, and then be alert to the thought patterns that develop in your mind.

The second step is to exercise your decision-making abilities. You have the right and the ability to reject any thought that comes to your mind.

What happens when the enemy attacks your mind? The thought enters into your mind and goes through a decision-making process. That is why you have a mind, be-

12

cause it makes decisions about who goes into the city. When you hear that thought, "You are a failure," your mind has a decision-making process to complete:

"Do I *receive* this thought? Do I *believe* this thought?"

Your mind will then search like a computer to see if any information concerning this thought has been filed away. If it has, and you have been accustomed to accepting thoughts like, "You are a failure," then you are going to have to make a conscious decision to reject that thought. Because you have accepted it, that thought is filed to always be accepted. You will have to *deprogram* it. It can be removed over a period of time by continually rejecting the thought and counteracting it with the Word of God. Declare out loud:

"I am a *success* because I meditate and act upon God's Word."

(See Joshua 1:8 and Psalm 1:2,3.) Continually rejecting the words of the enemy and accepting and declaring the Word of God will *reprogram* the computer of your mind. It will also exercise your decision-making ability and train it to accept the good and reject the evil.

Chapter 3
The Decision-Making Process

The decision-making process is what we must constantly guard, to be certain that our "walls" are in order. If you get lazy and don't exercise that God-given ability to reject the thoughts bombarding your mind, your walls will be broken down, your city will be ruined — and you will be a basket case.

"Well, I just can't help it. I'm an emotional person." That's all right. We are all emotional people. God gave us emotions, but they are not to rule us; we are to rule them. What you feel is a direct result of what you think. Whatever the emotion is — anger, fear, sorrow, grief — all the emotions we experience are a direct result of what we think. Your emotions are not something that overtakes you without any warning.

You may say, "I can't help it. This just happens to me; this is the way I am."

No. You rule over your own spirit. You

rule over your own emotions. And you do it by sorting through the thoughts that come to your mind. Thank God for our minds. Emotionally healthy people are people who can think clearly and make the right decisions about the thoughts that come into their mind. Do you want to know why people end up in the pits of depression? It is because they do not guard their mind.

Protect Your Heart

My son, attend to my words; incline thine ear unto my sayings.

Let them not depart from thine eyes; keep them in the midst of thine heart.

For they are life unto those that find them, and health to all their flesh.

Keep thy heart with all diligence; for out of it are the issues of life.

Proverbs 4:20-23

Let us study this Scripture. The word "keep" is used today as a very passive word. If we ask someone to "keep" something, we usually mean to "hold it until I get back." However, if you look it up in the Hebrew, it means "to guard and to protect with everything you have."

You say, "Well, God is going to protect me from these things." No, you are to protect your own spirit. You are to rule over your own spirit. And the Word of God tells us in this Scripture that we should guard our mind and our heart above everything else. We should give all diligence to protecting our city by being diligent to guard our thought life.

Depression

How does a person fall into the depths of depression?

I have had people tell me, "It just comes over me, and I don't know what happens."

Another person may say, "I can't control my emotions. I cry all the time. I just can't help it." There is nothing wrong with crying. It is only when you can't control your emotions that you enter a dangerous area.

You must constantly monitor your decision-making process by checking up on your thought patterns. If you let your mind wander and do anything it wants to, you are not in control of your spirit. You can't let it feed on soap operas, adultery, sickness, and disease. If you allow these things to pass through your gates and go into your inner city, you will be ruined. You will have holes in your wall!

This is what happens to people who fall into the depths of depression. They say they don't know what happens, but something *does* happen. A thought comes into their mind. For example, at work someone makes the offhanded remark, "The job you did yesterday was not done right, and you're going to have to do it over again this morning."

No one said, "You're a failure; They said, "You'll need to do it again; it wasn't done properly." The thoughts come into your mind:

"You're a failure; you never do anything right."

"Everything you do is wrong."

"How could you be so stupid?"

When those thoughts come into your mind and you dwell on them, you begin to feel that you are a failure. Not only do you *think* it; you *feel* it. And the more you feel it, the more you think it; and the more you think it, the more you feel it — until it overcomes you. Soon you are in the pits of depression. You say, "It just came over me. I don't know what happened."

Because your mind had already been

programmed, it accepted those thoughts as being true, and eventually depression was produced. If you had been guarding your thoughts, your decision-making process would have been exercised, and it would have rejected those thoughts. We need to monitor and guard the decision-making process diligently. Otherwise, it will become flabby, just like a muscle that's not used, and it will begin to deteriorate. And soon it will lose its power to decide, "No, I reject that thought."

And not only do you now have a hole in your wall, but the walls are beginning to crumble. One thought, one statement, "You're a failure," and the next thing that happens, everything that is said to you is negative and causes your depression to become deeper.

Guard your walls. Keep a check on your mind. What is happening in the soul realm? Keep a check on your decision-making process. Satan knows if he can get past those walls and get to your inner man, he can destroy you!

Chapter 4
Wounded and Broken Spirits Produce Physical Sickness

It is so important that you protect your heart and your spirit. Once your spirit has become crushed and broken, your emotions will be totally out of control.

A sound heart is the life of the flesh: but envy the rottenness of the bones.

Proverbs 14:30

Many people are physically sick today because they have problems in the emotional realm! Sickness often begins because of a broken spirit. Depressed and discouraged people do not stay healthy for long. A *sound* heart is the life of the flesh. Too many times we have gotten things out of order. We say, "Well, if they get healed, everything else will be all right."

It could be that the physical affliction is simply

a symptom of a soulish problem that has not been dealt with. It is interesting to study the stress test you can take to see if you are at high risk for sickness. Such things as divorce, death of a loved one, or losing a job are all emotionally explosive situations. These are said to bring a high risk of sickness.

> **The spirit of a man will sustain his infirmity; but a wounded spirit who can bear it?**
>
> **Proverbs 18:14**

A man's spirit, when it is strong, will sustain many physical wounds. We all know of people who because of their illness should have been dead, but because of their strong spirit, they lived. However, when a person's spirit is wounded, he can't handle anything else. Even the most insignificant problem seems overwhelming.

You can be physically weak, but if your spirit is strong, eventually your body will get well. But when your spirit is broken, and hopelessness, hurt, disappointment, and rejection take over, you can be destroyed not only emotionally, but physically.

> **A merry heart doeth good like a medicine: but a broken spirit drieth the bones.**
>
> **Proverbs 17:22**

When your spirit is broken, it can affect your physical body in many ways. Many emotionally ill people are being treated with drugs because their brain chemicals are out of balance. Medical science takes the view that many cases of paranoia and schizophrenia are a result of chemical imbalance. I believe that is possible, but I also question if the emotional state some people are in has actually *created* that chemical imbalance.

When your spirit is wounded, the chemicals in your body will be affected and will change. Your heart may beat faster, or your blood pressure may go up, among other changes. In order for you to stay well, your soulish area must prosper and be healthy also. The walls of your soul must be built up with no holes so that your spirit is continually protected.

Guard Your Spirit From the Attacks of People

When I first went into the ministry, it is a miracle that I was not destroyed. I did not know how to keep my walls up and repaired. I thought, "Here I am in the middle of God's will, doing what I'm supposed to do. Therefore, everything should be wonderful. Everyone will love me. It is just wonderful being in the center of God's will."

I didn't have my walls up to protect my spirit, and I took quite a bit of verbal abuse before I learned that everything was *not* so wonderful. My decision-making power had slipped, and wasn't exercised too well. After a meeting I would walk off the platform, excited about what God had done, and someone would say, "I don't believe a word you said, and I don't believe in women preachers. Don't you know you are going to hell for preaching, since you're a woman?"

(Order Charles Trombley's book, *Who Said Women Can't Teach?*, for a complete teaching on this subject.)

Even worse things than that were said, but I am not going to repeat them. I didn't know what to say. I was not prepared. My walls weren't up. I didn't know how to deal with it. I knew it was not right, but all the joy of what God had done in that meeting was gone, and I went into deep depression over it. I was allowing other people to govern my emotions.

Don't Let Others Take Over Your City

We *can* be ruled by other people. If your walls are down, people can march in and take over your city! It happened to me. I found that my entire life was being ruled by the fact that someone once told me that women shouldn't preach. And because I didn't have my gates and walls guarded, I fell into depression, discouragement, and defeat. My walls were down, and someone else took over my city.

I eventually learned with the help of the Holy Spirit to stop discouraging words from destroying me. I experienced freedom when I dealt with truth and not the lies of the enemy. *Everyone* did not hate me, but there were some who disliked me intensely! It was liberating to realize that some people will like me and encourage me, and some people won't. Once I learned this, I was prepared to deal with those who tried to knock holes in my walls.

Did you know that small holes get bigger as time goes along? The problem can start with just a little piece of mortar missing. But if you're not diligent and don't get that little hole repaired, it's going to get bigger and bigger and bigger. People who have constant problems with depression started that cycle with a few holes in the wall. Then their gates and walls were knocked down by discouragement, and depression invaded their city. No gates are left, so they quit making decisions to reject negative thoughts.

Practical Steps To Rid Yourself of Emotional Problems

You need to exercise your decision-making ability until it's strong, strong, strong. You can exercise it until, when someone says something discouraging to you, you will instantly compare it with the Word of God. Then you can say, "God did not say that about me; the Word didn't say that about me; and Jesus doesn't believe that about me. So I reject it!" And you can go on your way and never think about it again.

At first, it is like when you begin aerobics. Have you ever tried to do the exercises they show on television? About the time you have learned one move, they are doing something else! It takes muscle strength and coordination.

Exercising your decision-making ability is very similar. It takes daily practice. You may find yourself in the middle of the day feeling down and depressed. At the very moment you realize you are depressed, you must stop and say, "Why do I feel this way?"

Step One: *"Why do I feel this way?"*

Something has happened to cause this feeling. A thought entered your mind; an alien came past your walls into your city! If you feel depressed, there is an alien in your city. The minute you have that funny feeling, stop and say, "What thought came into my mind? What happened that caused me to have this feeling?"

If you have a difficult time discerning the thoughts that caused your depression, ask the Holy Spirit to show you, and He will.

Step Two: *"Holy Spirit, I ask for your help. Reveal to me the source of my feelings."*

I have found it is very helpful to ask yourself *when* you began to feel down and depressed. After locating the general time, recall any conversations that took place or incidents that were negative. It could have been a subtle thought that came as a result of a *very* insignificant incident. However, that one thought triggered an entire file of negative thought patterns in your mind.

Step Three: *"When did I first begin to feel this way?"*

The moment you discover that thought pattern, command it to leave your mind. Immediately say, "I will not let that affect me." Because your mind was programmed from the past to accept that thought as truth, it slipped past your gate and into your heart. When it got to your heart, you felt it. So just slide it right back outside the door and get rid of it.

Step Four: *"I reject these thoughts in Jesus' Name."*

At this point, you must deal with the truth. What is the truth? The truth is what the Word of God says about you. Begin to declare God's Word, speaking boldly in Jesus' Name:

> **I am the righteousness of God in Christ.**
>
> **2 Corinthians 5:21**
>
> **There is no condemnation to me, because I am in Christ Jesus.**
>
> **Romans 8:1**
>
> **God has not given me a spirit of fear.**
>
> **2 Timothy 1:7**
>
> **I am accepted, not rejected. I am accepted in Him.**
>
> **Ephesians 1:6**
>
> **I am successful because I obey God's Word.**
>
> **Joshua 1:8**

Step Five: *"I am who God says I am!"*

You can do this with depression, rejection, fear, or anything else that attacks your mind. Over a period of time as you continue to practice this exercise, you will catch the thoughts more quickly. Instead of being depressed or dejected for a day, a week, or months, it will be hours, then minutes, then seconds. It will get to the point that when a negative thought comes to your mind, or you have that feeling, you will reject it, and it will disappear instantly.

Eventually, when the thought hits your mind, you will get rid of it so fast you'll never even have the *feeling* that usually comes with negative thoughts.

Don't think this will happen overnight. It takes diligent work to keep the wall in repair. Be diligent with your mind. As you practice this exercise, you will see great improvement in your feelings.

Don't be condemned if you are in an emotional mess right now. Start where you are. As you begin to take authority over the thoughts that enter your mind, you can repair your walls and get your heart healed.

Addictions: A Spiritual Problem

I know many people who have tried to cover the pain of a broken heart with alcohol, drugs, or even food. Because their pain is temporarily alleviated, they become addicted. Addiction is no answer to a broken spirit. It only enhances the problems. Patching the holes in your wall with bandaids will not solve any problems.

I'm not giving you a formula to heal these

hurts and wounds in your life. What I am saying is that the Spirit of God can heal you through the Word of God. Too many people have gone after healing the wrong way. The Holy Spirit is the only One who knows you personally enough to know how you're going to be healed in the area of your emotions. Yes, God does use other people. But you are going to have to open yourself wide to the Holy Spirit. It is the Word that ministers life to your spirit. As your emotional problems are healed, the need for any "crutches" will leave.

Chapter 5
Don't Expect Others To Heal Your Hurts

Many of us have had our walls broken down by people who hurt and rejected us. It could be family, friends, or a spouse. The walls are broken down, and we want the person who broke the walls down to repair them for us. If a city is attacked by the enemy and ravished on the inside, you don't expect the enemy to return to refurbish the city and rebuild the walls! It just doesn't happen. The person who hurt and injured you cannot repair your wall for you. It does not matter if he apologizes, repents, gets on his knees, and begs your forgiveness — you have to repair your own walls.

You may feel better about that person, but because of the rejection you experienced, you will begin to expect rejection from other people as well. Consequently, you will be open to the onslaught of the enemy. You must repair your own walls after you've been attacked.

You ask, "How can I do that?"

It's your responsibility, but you have help. When Jesus left, He said, "I leave you a Comforter, a Counselor, an Intercessor, an Advocate, a Standby, One who will be with you, and teach you all things, and guide you into all truth." We've thought that the Holy Spirit was sent only to reveal truths of the Word of God, but the Holy Spirit will show you how to repair walls in your life that have been broken down by others. He will also *help* you repair those walls. The Holy Spirit does not take over and do the work for you. He is a Helper.

Do you know what a carpenter's helper does? He helps. He doesn't do the carpentry; he helps. That is what the Holy Spirit does. He will come and show you exactly how you can repair the holes that are in your wall. The Holy Spirit is by far the best Teacher when it comes to the emotional realm. He knows everything about us. Jesus sent Him to assist us in every area. Being full of the Holy Spirit, Jesus is a perfect example of a man who refused to relinquish control of His emotions.

You Don't Have To Be Destroyed by Your Emotions

Somehow we've had the idea that Jesus walked the face of the earth only experiencing the emotions of love and compassion. But Jesus experienced the entire range of human emotions.

> **For we have not an high priest which cannot be touched with the feeling of our infirmities; but was in all points tempted like as we are, yet without sin.**
>
> **Hebrews 4:15**

Jesus experienced every human emotion that we have ever experienced — rejection, discouragement, the opportunity for depression and fear — yet He was not destroyed by His emotions. And you don't have to be destroyed by yours, either!

Jesus said:

> **The Spirit of the Lord is upon me, because he hath anointed me to preach the gospel to the poor; he hath sent me to heal the brokenhearted, to preach deliverance to the captives, and recovering of sight to the blind, to set at liberty them that are bruised.**
>
> **Luke 4:18**

I've meditated and prayed, "God, we see the blind eyes opened; we see the lame walk; we see those who are in bondage to sin, drugs, and alcohol set free — but where is the healing of the brokenhearted today?" There are more brokenhearted people in the Body of Christ now than ever.

Of course, some people don't want to be healed. That hurt and rejection has become a close personal friend of theirs. They want to hold onto it so they can continue to get sympathy from other people. The sympathy feels good for a while, but eventually it becomes miserable. If you've had that problem, let go of it. Open yourself to God. Your deliverance is more important than a short period of enjoying the sympathy of others. The joy you have in ministering healing to others after you have been delivered will be a thousand times greater than a little sympathy.

Stand in the Gap

We, as the Body of Christ, need to stand in the gap for the healing of the brokenhearted. Thank God for the Holy Spirit who is our Helper — but we also need the Body of Christ. We are members one of another, and when one suffers, we all suffer. We need the Body of Christ to help us to repair our walls after they've been broken down many times.

If you have had emotional problems and instability in your life, you need to be in a stable church that is teaching the Word of God. You will not be able to receive healing of an emotional instability by flitting from one meeting to another. You need the constant help and support of the local Body of Christ. That stability will help you build your walls back up again. I don't mean you attend only once a month, either. Go everytime the doors are open, and receive from a pastor who has a heart for his people. The love of God that is ministered under the anointing of a God-called pastor will help heal the hurts in your life.

We need to lend our prayers and stand in the gap for others. When the wall is broken down and there is a big gap, someone needs to stand there and protect the city until the wall is rebuilt. You and the Holy Spirit are going to be there laying the bricks and the mortar, but when you have a hole here and there, and a whole wall section down somewhere else, you are going to need some help while you're laying those bricks so fast. That's when we, as the Body of Christ, can support and can help one another. We need to stand guard against the enemy while our friends are repairing their walls. This can be done by intercession and emotional support.

Emotional *support* does not mean emotional *dependency*. We need to depend, first of all, upon the Spirit of God. God is the only One who can meet every need in your life. But don't shut yourself off from the Body of Christ, because there is help there also. We are representatives of Christ, to minister reconciliation to each other. Jesus paid the supreme sacrifice for the sins of every person. Withholding His forgiveness and love from a person can keep them bound.

In ministering to people who have struggled over and over with sin in their life, God showed me that I was to be a minister of reconciliation. These people have tried in their own strength to overcome sin. They loved God, but they couldn't accept themselves, because they continually fell back into the same sin. They could not forgive themselves, and they did not know how to receive forgiveness from God. The condemnation that resulted kept them in the same dilemma. Although they prayed, "God forgive me," they could not receive forgiveness from God, because they did not know how. This is emotionally destructive. As a minister of reconciliation, I could stand in the gap and demonstrate the forgiveness of God to them.

When these emotionally devastated people would confess to me that they had sinned again, I did not react by adding to their condemnation. Instead of saying, "I can't believe it — here we prayed and believed God, and you didn't have enough faith. Straighten your act up. That's all it takes. Put that bottle down and do not drink anymore; just quit it!" How easy it is to let those words "Just quit" come out of our mouth. That is like looking at someone in the depths of depression and saying, "Well, just quit being depressed!" If it were that easy, we would all be slim, trim, strong, and disciplined.

To be a minister of reconciliation, you must release people from condemnation so they feel free to go to God with their problems. Many times I have said,

"It is all right. I forgive you."

"But now you are going to do better."

"We are going to pray, and you are going to receive the forgiveness of God."

They could not receive the love and forgiveness from Jesus at that point, so I had to stand in the gap and minister forgiveness and love to them.

Each time there came a confidence in that person's spirit that "God has forgiven me. I am worthy because Jesus made me worthy."

One person told me, "I had never experienced the love and forgiveness of God. I didn't know how to receive it until I experienced it through you, and now I am able to receive it from the Lord."

We are to be ministers of reconciliation. You should protect yourself from people, but that does not mean you shut everyone out all the time. All it means is that you protect your heart. You love people with the love of God, but you do not open your inner city to any "alien" who walks by. Keep your hurt from becoming emotional devastation.

Jesus experienced hurt from being rejected. He experienced anger. He experienced the same emotions we do, but they never destroyed him. It is because the love of God is more powerful than any hurt or any rejection.

Get Rid of the Aliens

If aliens have entered into your inner city, you need to get rid of them. What are some of the aliens? Unforgiveness, bitterness, depression, rejection, guilt, fear, and sin are all aliens. Once they have come into your city, they will destroy it. You need to get rid of them. How do you do that? First, you confess it to the Father; then you rebuke them in Jesus' Name.

The only thing that should be dwelling in your city is the fruit of the spirit: love, joy, peace, long-suffering, goodness, meekness, faith, and temperance. Let the fruit of the spirit dwell in you. If you have aliens in your city you will have to make the decision to get rid of them and start rebuilding your walls.

Pray this prayer with me:

Heavenly Father, I confess that I have allowed aliens to enter my city. I ask You to cleanse my heart right now from all unrighteousness. I command all fear, bitterness, rejection, and sin to depart from me now. I ask that the healing power of Jesus Christ would flow through my mind and emotions and heal me now. From this hour forward, I will guard my heart with all diligence, in Jesus' Name.

Chapter 6
Reverse the Curse
of Sickness

Now that the emotional areas of your life have been dealt with, and you have removed the hindrances of sin and bitterness, God can bring healing to your physical body. Before this can be done, however, we need to establish some facts in your mind concerning God's will for your healing.

Sickness Is a Curse

The first thing we want to establish is that *sickness is a curse.* It is not a blessing! In some religious circles over the years, it has been a popular belief that God causes sickness to come upon His people in order to teach them things, or in order that they may grow spiritually. No greater lie has ever been told! If that is so, then sickness is a blessing from God, and we should never attempt to get rid of a blessing! If that is so, we shouldn't go to doctors, visit hospitals, or take medication — even aspirin! To do so would rob us of a *blessing* and to be healed would be a *curse*.

Some say, "Well, if I got healed, I might not serve God. Perhaps I would turn away from godliness. So, this sickness is a blessing."

I would never want those words to come out of my mouth. *Do not reverse the blessing trying to make it a curse.* The Word of God is very definite in Acts 10:38 that sickness is an oppression of the devil. Sickness is from the devil, and healing is from Jesus Christ. No exceptions. Until there are no exceptions in your mind and your understanding, you will not be able to receive healing from the Word of God. You may be healed in a miracle service where the gifts of healings are in operation, but you will not be able to receive healing from the Word. Why? Because if there is an area of doubt in your mind, it will be a hindrance to receiving healing.

The leper in Matthew 8:2,3 had doubts concerning Jesus' willingness to heal. As soon as Jesus said, "I *will*; be thou clean," the leper was healed. The doubt first had to be removed from the leper's mind. Sickness is a curse. If you don't believe it, maybe we should ask the woman with the issue of blood.

> **And a certain woman, which had an issue of blood twelve years,**
>
> **And had suffered many things of many physicians, and had spent all that she had, and was nothing bettered, but rather grew worse,**
>
> **When she had heard of Jesus, came in the press behind, and touched his garment.**
>
> **For she said, If I may touch but his clothes, I shall be whole.**
>
> Mark 5:25-28

For twelve years she had been sick. And for twelve years she had been to many physicians and had suffered many things. Sometimes their cures were worse than the problem.

She spent all the money she had, but she didn't get better. Instead, she grew worse. How many people in the world today have spent every cent they had trying to be healed; trying to find someone who could help them.

Sickness is a curse, not only to the body, but to the pocketbook. Many have been financially ruined because of sickness. It is a *curse* to the people who are sick, because they can spend all they have. They may be wealthy in the beginning, not under the curse of poverty, but by the end of their disease, they may be poverty stricken, with nothing left. *Sickness is a curse!*

Sickness is also a curse to the family of the sick person. Have you ever known a family who has a loved one with a terminal or a debilitating illness in their home? If you have not, I can tell you what happens. I have seen it many times. The entire family is surrounded by the problem, and they become consumed by it in their thought life. They are emotionally devastated. It is a curse to the emotions, because there is no peace. Their time is consumed in caring for the sick person. They suffer because the loved one suffers. Does that sound like God's blessing on the household?

Perhaps you think, "Well, I know God heals, but some people have gotten saved because of illness."

There *have* been those who were born again in spite of the fact that Satan tried to kill or maim them, but they did not have to get sick to get saved. That is not a requirement, and it is not in the Word of God.

Sickness is *not* a blessing in any shape, form, or fashion. It is a curse. So do not reverse the blessings of God.

Chapter 7
Doctors Cannot Reverse the Curse

Doctors cannot reverse the curse. They can help alleviate some pain and suffering, but they cannot reverse the curse of sickness. They can only assist the body in healing. The curse stops the body's natural healing process. Say aloud:

"Sickness is a curse. Sickness is not from God."

There are many verses in the Bible proving that sickness always originates from the devil; not from God.

Have you ever had a relative who was sick? Did you want that person sick? Then how could we, as human beings, imperfect as we are, want our children, parents, sisters, brothers, or cousins sick? If we desire with all of our heart to see them well and whole, how can we expect anything *less* from God? Our human love is not on the level of God's love. God's love far surpasses human love. If we do not want to see our loved ones suffer, how much more does God not want to see us suffer? How much more does He want us well? Say this:

"God wants me well."

It would not have been so bad if the woman with the issue of blood had received a little help and felt better. But no, it says that she spent everything she had on physicians and was not better, but worse. She surely must have been discouraged after twelve years of seeking help and growing worse. The physicians she went to wanted to help her, just as doctors today desire to help people, but there is only so much they can do.

But something happened that encouraged this woman and lifted her faith to seek Jesus for healing. She surely heard the testimony of someone else who touched Jesus and was healed of their disease. Have you ever heard of someone being healed and been encouraged when you needed healing in your own body? This woman heard a testimony, and it encouraged her, because she said:

If I may touch but his clothes, I shall be whole.

Mark 5:28

Place Your Sickness on Jesus

This woman faced a major problem. For her to touch Jesus would be to defile Him. Under the law, a woman in her condition was not to appear in public, because she would defile people. But she said, "If I can touch Him, I will be whole."

Somewhere in this woman's heart, in the depths of her spirit, she had a revelation of what was going to happen to Jesus: He was going to take upon Himself the defilement of all the diseases known to mankind. Not only the diseases, but the defilement of sin would come upon Him, the pure, sinless Son of God. Somewhere in the depths of her spirit she understood, *Himself took our infirmities, and bare our sicknesses* (Matt. 8:17). Jesus took her infirmities upon Himself. As that woman touched His garment, the Word says that virtue went out of Him.

I see here a picture of the substitutionary work of Jesus Christ. He became her Substitute. She placed upon Him, by that touch of faith, the sickness that had ravaged her body for twelve years. By that touch, she not only *received* the virtue, or healing power, but she *placed* her sickness upon His body, where it belonged. She gave it over to Him.

In the Old Testament, the priest would

lay his hands upon the head of the scapegoat and confess over him all the iniquities of the children of Israel. (See Leviticus 16:21.) In touching the goat, they conferred or placed their sins upon it, and they went away clean. The scapegoat then went out into the wilderness to meet its death. This was a type of the Lord Jesus Christ. He was our Substitute and our scapegoat. He bore our sins and sicknesses away on His cross. In the same manner, the women touched and placed her sickness and disease upon the Lamb of God, and left it there. He became sick that we might be made well!

You say, "Oh, I can't understand all that."

Can you understand the emotions involved when someone says, "I just wish I could bear this sickness for my loved one. I would rather be sick myself than watch him suffer." It is impossible in the natural realm for a doctor or anyone else to reverse the curse, because they cannot take the sickness on themselves to set you free. But in Jesus Christ it was possible. He bore it so you don't have to!

I don't understand all of it, either. I can understand what the Bible teaches, but I can't understand how our sicknesses and diseases could be placed upon His body by the stripes He suffered. However, the important part is not that we *understand* the workings of every bit of it, but that we *believe* it. If God's Word says it, we must believe it. I do not completely understand salvation, either, but I believed it, and I received it!

Do you believe if you confess Jesus as the Lord of your life, believing His blood was shed for you, that you will be saved? Are you totally convinced of it? Suppose someone came to Jesus and said, "I am a sinner. I need Jesus. Lord, forgive me. I receive your blood to cleanse me from all unrighteousness." Would you doubt that that person could be saved? If you are born again, I know your reply would be, "Of course not! I *know* they would receive salvation!"

What if a Christian came before the throne of grace and said, "I am sick, and I need to accept Jesus as my Great Physician." Do you believe he would be healed? Do you have any doubts? Your answer is probably a less emphatic "yes" than with salvation. We have been well programmed with the Word of God about salvation, but not about healing.

We have also been programmed to believe that doctors will help us. If they give us instructions, we follow them, because we have faith in doctors. If we had as much faith in God that we have in doctors, we would see many more healings.

We do have faith in the shed blood of Jesus Christ, because it has been emphasized and taught in most churches for years. If you were raised in a church, you heard it taught in Sunday School. If anyone witnessed to you, they told you that you could be saved and become a new creature in Christ Jesus. Because we heard it so often, the repetition caused us to have faith and confidence in the ability of the Lord Jesus Christ's shed blood to cleanse us from all unrighteousness. We have no problem in our mind with His willingness to save anyone who comes to Him.

As we hear more teaching on healing through the Atonement of Jesus Christ, our faith and confidence will grow in this area also. We will answer emphatically, "Yes. All who come to Jesus for healing will be healed!"

Chapter 8
The Double Curse — The Double Cure

We need to stress the fact that our salvation and our healing were accomplished *at the very same time*. Sin and sickness are the double curse!

When Adam sinned, he received the curse of spiritual death. Spiritual death cut off his life force from God, and physical death began. Adam's sin also brought about the curse of sickness. Sickness is an attack to weaken and kill the body.

I am endeavoring to show you from the Word of God that your healing was bought and paid for by the Lord Jesus Christ at the very same time that your salvation was. I want you to grasp this great truth. If you need healing in your body, please do not read this half-heartedly. If a doctor were talking to you and said, "Now, I have something that will make you totally well," you would give your full attention to what that doctor said. But that doctor cannot reverse the curse — and the Word of God can. So pay attention with everything you have to grasp the truths I'm teaching here.

> **He is despised and rejected of men; a man of sorrows, and acquainted with grief: and we hid as it were our faces from him; he was despised, and we esteemed him not.**
>
> **Isaiah 53:3**

Here, Isaiah is prophesying about Jesus. He said *"He is despised and rejected of men, a man of sorrows."* If you look into the Hebrew, you will find that this was mistranslated into modern English. When we think of "sorrow" today, we think of someone who is upset over a friend or a loved one, or is sorrowful about something. The word "sorrow" is actually the word "pain." Why was Jesus a man of pain? Because He bore our pain. He took it upon Himself. "And acquainted with grief." The word "grief" is another unfortunate translation. It does not mean grief as we know it. It means, "He was acquainted with sickness and disease." Why was Jesus acquainted with sickness and disease? It was not because He was sickly, but because He took our sickness and disease upon Himself.

> **Surely he hath borne our griefs,**

and carried our sorrows: ye[...]
esteem him stricken, smitten[...]
and afflicted.

Isaia[...]

What did Jesus bear? The Word sa[...]
bore our pain! Is there any question in y[...]
mind that the Word of God is an establishe[...]
fact? It is forever established in the heavens,
and it is the basis for our Christian belief.
Right here, on the printed page, the Word of
God says, "He hath borne our sickness and
diseases."

The Double Curse Carried Away

The word "borne" means, "to lift up,
bear away, and remove to a distance." Just
as the scapegoat went into the wilderness,
carrying sin, never to be seen again, so Jesus
has "carried away, borne away, our sickness
and our disease. He has carried them away."

You may be thinking: "Yes, but I'm still
sick!"

Is the Word of God true or not? If it is true
— and I believe with all my heart it is true —
then it says, "Jesus carried away our sicknesses and our diseases, and our pain." He
removed them from us. *"Yet we did esteem him
stricken, smitten of God, and afflicted. But he was
wounded for our transgressions. . . . "*

What are "transgressions"? Sins, right? "He was wounded for our transgressions, or sins. He was bruised for our iniquities, or sins." Do you believe that part of the Scripture? If we went to some churches, they would definitely believe that Scripture, and even preach on it every Sunday of the year, but they would not preach *the rest of it*.

Yes, He bore our transgressions and our iniquities, but read the rest of the verse: *"the chastisement of our peace was upon him; and with his stripes we are healed."* Some will quote that as, "With his stripes *some* are healed. *Some* occasionally will be healed. *Some have been healed.*" No! This is a settled, established fact: "With His stripes we *are* (present tense) healed."

> Yet it pleased the Lord to bruise him; he hath put him to grief: when thou shall make his soul an offering for sin, he shall see his seed, he shall prolong his days, and the pleasure of the Lord shall prosper in his hand.
>
> He shall see the travail of his soul, and be satisfied: by his knowledge shall my righteous servant justify many, for he shall bear their iniquities.
>
> Isaiah 53:10,11

The word "bear" is the same word that is

brought out in verse four and serves as a theme for the rest of this chapter: "He hath borne our griefs (or pain)." Jesus bore our sins, our iniquities. At the very same time, He also bore our sicknesses, our diseases, and our pain. Throughout the Word of God there is no separation of the two in the Atonement of the Lord Jesus Christ.

When Jesus bore our sins to make it possible for us to be saved and be a new creature in Christ Jesus, He also bore in His body our sicknesses and diseases so we might be whole, well, and healed. At the same moment that He was bruised for our sins, He took the stripes on His back for our healing.

Sick Christians

Some say, "But you know there are a lot of sick Christians!" It is obvious there are many sick in the Body of Christ. I cannot give you only one reason for the number of sick Christians, but I can tell you why many in the Body of Christ are sick. I believe Paul gave us the answer in First Corinthians 11:

> **For he that eateth and drinketh unworthily, eateth and drinketh damnation to himself, not discerning the Lord's body.**
>
> **For this cause many are weak and sickly among you, and many sleep.**
> **1 Corinthians 11:29,30**

Paul said it was from "not discerning the Lord's body." And he said, "For this cause many are weak and sickly among you." What does that mean? He did not say it was from not discerning the Lord's blood. They were discerning that the *blood* washed away their sins, but they were not discerning that His *body* was broken for us, so we might be healed.

We have emphasized salvation in the blood of Jesus, but how many times, in comparison, have we emphasized that Jesus bore our sicknesses and diseases at the very same time? How often have we been taught that salvation of the soul and physical healing of the body happened *at the same time?* How many times have we heard that? Not enough, obviously; not nearly enough.

If it is true that Jesus bore our sicknesses at the same time that He bore our sins, why are many sitting in church born again, but sick? It's because we have not had enough repetition of these Scriptures to establish confidence in our hearts. We need as much confidence in healing as we have in salvation. When we arrive at that point, we will see people coming to be born again who will be instantly healed. They will be healed just as they are saved, because they will be told,

"Come here and accept Jesus, and you will be healed instantly." We do not expect that now, but we should.

Let's look at the argument, "If Jesus bore away sickness and disease at Calvary, why aren't all Christians healed?" Let's turn it around: "If Jesus bore away sin and iniquity at Calvary, why are people still unsaved?" Why is everyone not born again? It is because they do not receive and accept salvation. Isn't that true? All it takes to receive forgiveness of your sins is to accept and receive what Jesus did. Isn't that true?

All Christians do not accept Jesus as their Healer when they are born again. As a matter of fact, many Christians *never* accept the fact that the stripes placed on Jesus' back were for *their* healing. This is the same basic reason people die and go to hell: They refuse to believe what Jesus did on the cross, or they are ignorant of what Jesus did. Our only cure to keep Christians from being sick is to get rid of ignorance concerning healing and unbelief.

You will never hear me say flippantly, "Well, the reason you didn't receive your healing is because you don't have enough faith." If you *believe* what God's Word says, you will have faith. If you don't have enough faith, it's because of a lack of knowledge of the Word, or refusing to accept what it says.

Chapter 9
Roadblocks to Healing

There are roadblocks to healing, even when you have a knowledge of God's Word and have accepted healing as an established fact.

I have been in the ministry fourteen years, and I have taught healing all that time. Yet there have been times in my own life that I have not been able to receive my healing immediately. I knew one thing: It wasn't a lack of knowledge. I could quote almost every Scripture in the Bible on healing! I believe it. I believe in healing, yet I was sick. I came to this conclusion: My inability to receive healing was no reflection on what was done in Jesus Christ.

Not one time that I was sick did I ever say, "Maybe healing is not for me. Maybe healing doesn't work. Maybe it is not true. Maybe Jesus didn't bear our sicknesses." Not one time did I say that, because I *knew* the Word said the opposite. My personal experience did not make the word of God untrue. Healing *was* accomplished by Jesus on Calvary, and no matter who gets healed or who does not get healed, it is an established fact. If I have not received my healing, it is because of some roadblock Satan has sent to hinder my acceptance of it. I'm not talking about a lack of faith. I believe in the Word. I had faith, but there was an inability to receive — there was a roadblock.

Don't ever think that the path to healing and divine health is going to be easy! It is strewn with roadblocks to trip you. There I stood, a minister of the Word of God, teaching on divine healing, yet for some reason there was a roadblock in my path — an inability to receive healing.

So what did I do — cry? I was tempted to call every spiritual person I knew and ask them to pray for me. Instead, I went to God. *He* knows *all* the answers. I said, "God, there is some reason why I have not been able to receive this healing." I didn't put the blame on myself. Too many people turn on themselves and say, "Well, I'm just not strong enough spiritually. I don't have enough faith. I guess I'm just one of those people with little faith."

Someone is always so ready to come

along, join with your self-condemnation, and say, "Well, if you just had enough faith, your child wouldn't have died. If you had enough faith, your husband would not have gotten sick. If you had enough faith, you would not be sick now. You must not be reading the Word enough."

Instead of spending so much time on *introspection*, spend more time *inspecting* the Word of God!

> **There is therefore now no con-
> demnation to them which are in
> Christ Jesus, who walk not after the
> flesh, but after the Spirit.**
>
> **Romans 8:1**

God is not condemning you. Satan is the one who condemns.

After digging out from under self-condemnation, I began to discuss my problem with God, because He is the one who knows what the problem is.

I said, "God, You know there is a roadblock here. There is something that is hindering. I do not know what it is. Please show me."

The first thing many people have told me is, "Well, there is sin in your life. That is the reason you are sick." It could be true that when a person walks in sin, he walks away from the protection of God, but that is not always the case.

I prayed, "God, is there sin in my life?" He didn't say anything about it, and the Holy Spirit will always tell you if you are in sin.

The Sin of Omission

Then the Holy Spirit brought a sin of omission to my mind; something that God had wanted me to do, but I had procrastinated and did not do. I had put it off. So I immediately took care of it. I continued to pray. And my condition got worse!

Don't think that the devil is going to stand back once you make headway toward anything in God's Word. It is possible you could receive a miracle healing and never have another problem. But most people who become mature in the Word are going to have to *stand* on the Word of God and *fight* the good fight of faith. That's just a fact. If you are looking for something easy, you'll not find it. But receiving your healing through the fight of faith is still better than being sick.

One morning as I woke up, I said, without even thinking of the Scripture in Acts 16:30, "What must I do to be healed?" As I said that, the Spirit of God spoke to me and said, "Believe on the Lord Jesus Christ."

That is what Paul and Silas said to the Philippian jailer:

> **Believe on the Lord Jesus Christ, and thou shalt be saved, and thy house.**
>
> **Acts 16:31**

We should be able to accept healing and salvation as a complete package. The word "saved" is the Greek word *sozo*, which also means "to heal and make whole." Again and again it came to me, "Believe, believe, believe." What must I do? *Believe* on the Lord Jesus Christ."

Believe on what? The Spirit of God spoke, "Believe Jesus is Lord. Believe Jesus is Lord, Master, and Ruler over sickness, and it must depart at His Name! Believe that your sickness was placed upon Him. The symptoms that afflict your body, place over on Him. Believe that He bore your sickness and disease."

I can only speak of what has happened to me and how I received healing. I can't tell you how you are going to receive your healing. Every individual is different. There are no pat formulas; only principles. When we try to put everyone in one group and say,

"This is all you have to do. Just take these three steps, and you will be healed," it will not always work.

You can never put any five people into one category and expect them to be healed the same way, because they will not respond in the same manner. Only the Spirit of God knows what it will take for you to release *your* faith for healing, and He is very capable of transmitting that understanding to you.

When I began to ask God about my healing, to meditate on His Word, and to act on what He told me to do, the roadblocks started being removed. I believed that regardless of what was happening in my physical body, the Word of God was true — and I refused to be moved.

Discouragement

I became discouraged. I'll be honest with you. At one point I became *really* discouraged. It is easy to believe you are healed when you feel good. It is harder to believe you are healed when you can't even get up out of bed or move, and you're in such pain that you wish you could die. It is much easier to receive from God and believe when you are not in the middle of a crisis. That's why it's so important to listen closely to the

Word and stand on the Scriptures concerning healing *before* you are attacked with sickness.

Every Sunday, I dragged myself out of bed and went to church, because I needed to hear the Word of God. I made myself sit and listen to it, regardless of how I felt.

One Sunday morning as I woke up, a song about healing was playing over my clock radio, and I began to worship God. I felt the healing power of God manifest in that room. The anointing of God was all over my room! The healing process had begun, although I did not receive my total healing at that time.

Often, the answer comes in stages. Occasionally, it takes several stages from the beginning of healing to the total manifestation. There is nothing wrong with that. Do not be discouraged if you have not experienced a total manifestation of healing in your body. Keep following the stages to the very end. God will do everything He can to get that healing to you when you are believing Him.

I went to church with the anointing of God still on me. At the end of the service, my pastor said, "Annette, this is your day. Get up here." He laid hands on me, and immediately the symptoms that I'd been having left my body. It took a little longer for me to regain the strength that I'd had before, but the symptoms left.

I followed the stages that the Holy Spirit led me through to healing. He always leads you in line with God's Word, and He will always lead you down the path to healing and divine health.

Often, we talk about faith, trying to have faith, and trying to *work up* faith to be healed. I want you to lay hold on this one truth: *Believing is a choice you make.*

Chapter 10
Healing Is a Choice

You do not have to *try* to believe. Belief is a *choice*. People who believe in atheism do not work at trying to believe in atheism. They may study different religions and decide that atheism is what they believe. A person may, decide after hearing about Mormonism, "This is what I believe." They do not say, "Well, I am trying to believe in Mormonism." Belief is a choice.

Often we wonderful human beings try to believe according to what we *feel*. Do you love your husband, wife, children, or parents? If you said "yes" emphatically, it is because you *feel* like you love them. If you did not say anything, or you said it without conviction, you did so because you don't *feel* much love today. Perhaps you had a fight with them today. Tomorrow you may *feel* love again. But real love is a *choice* based on your *will* to love, not how you *feel*. Just because you don't feel love for your children one day does not mean that you put them up for adoption. Feelings are easily changed.

Belief is a choice, just as the God-kind of love is a choice. Human feelings change all the time. And your feelings about what you believe in the Word of God may change all the time, but *you must choose between your feelings and your beliefs*. You either choose to believe Jesus bore your sin and sickness at the same time, or you choose not to believe it. You choose to believe that you are healed, or you choose to believe you are not healed. *It is a choice*.

When you make that choice, that is your belief — regardless of what you feel like. You have chosen, and therefore you believe, regardless of what you feel like. You cannot base your beliefs on what you feel. If so, your beliefs would change every hour. You choose your *beliefs*, and then your *feelings* come in line with what you have chosen.

I call heaven and earth to record this day against you, that I have set before you life and death, blessing and cursing: therefore choose life, that both thou and thy seed may live.
Deuteronomy 30:19

It is your choice. It is simple. When you go to the grocery store, you may choose either chicken or beef, if those are your available choices. If you really like chicken, you'll say, "I'll take the chicken." You chose it. In regard to healing and salvation, you just choose. Which do you want: sickness or healing? You choose to believe on Jesus Christ for the healing of your body.

Thousands of us have chosen to believe upon Jesus Christ for salvation, but when it comes to healing, we have decided not to cast our ballot. You choose: one way or the other.

I challenge you this day: Choose what you believe. Choose to believe that Jesus bore your sicknesses, and with His stripes you are healed.

The curse of sin was death to the spirit of man. God told them, "If you eat of this tree, you will surely die" (Gen. 2:17). Upon Adam and Eve came the curse of death, which was spiritual death. If God had not allowed *physical* death to come as a result of *spiritual* death, man would have lived in that spiritually dead state of sin throughout eternity!

Could you imagine what it would be like if every horrible sinner who ever existed upon the face of the earth were still alive today? When God said that death would come, death came not only to the spiritual part of man, but also to the physical part of man. Of course, sickness is the beginning of death. That is the double curse: The curse of *sin* was spiritual death; the curse of *sickness* was *physical death*.

David said:

> **Bless the Lord, O my soul, and forget not all his benefits:**
>
> **Who forgiveth all thine iniquities; who healeth all thy diseases.**
>
> **Psalm 103:2,3**

Even Peter had a revelation of sin and sickness being swept away together:

> **Who his own self bare our sins in his own body on the tree, that we, being dead to sins, should live unto righteousness: by whose stripes ye were healed.**
>
> **1 Peter 2:24**

Sin and sickness are also connected by James:

> **Is any sick among you? let him call for the elders of the church; and let them pray over him, anointing him with oil in the name of the Lord:**
>
> **And the prayer of faith shall save the sick, and the Lord shall raise him up; and if he have committed sins, they shall be forgiven him.**
>
> **James 5:14,15**

We need to remember the latter part of the Scripture, which states that if you have sins in your life, they shall be forgiven you.

Resist Sickness As an Enemy

If you have sin in your life, repent first, and then you can receive your healing. We need to be taught to resist sickness as an enemy. We need to learn to resist sickness as we resist the temptation to sin. Sickness is not a friend. It's an enemy. It's a curse.

When we feel or sense sickness coming upon us, we should resist it just as we would resist the temptation to commit a sin of any kind. Take the shield of faith and resist the fiery darts of the enemy. The fiery darts that hit you could be symptoms of sickness. The shield of faith is to *stop* the darts from hitting you; not for pulling them out *after* they've hit.

We say, "Well, I'm using my faith. I have caught a terrible cold, and I'm using my faith to get rid of it." In doing so, you are trying to pull darts out with the shield of faith. No, the shield of faith is to be held in place at all times so you do not get hit. Use your faith to *live* in divine health. *Divine healing* is not the best. *Divine health* is the best.

Chapter 11
Your Curse Ended at Calvary

As the children of Israel wandered in the wilderness, they murmured and complained, and a curse came upon them. Serpents bit them, and they died. God told Moses to do a strange thing:

> **And Moses made a serpent of brass, and put it upon a pole, and it came to pass, that if a serpent had bitten any man, when he beheld the serpent of brass, he lived.**
>
> **Numbers 21:9**

The serpent on the pole was a type of Jesus on the cross!

How could that serpent be a type of Jesus Christ? Because Jesus took upon Himself sin on the cross and became sin for us. He became our Substitute. Not only did sin come upon Him, but judgment because of sin. The serpent was made out of brass, which is symbolic of judgment. That meant the judgment of

God was upon the sin. The curse came because of our sin and overtook Jesus. The curse destined for us came upon Him.

Moses told those who had been bitten to look upon the snake. What happens when you "look upon" something? You pay attention to it. You consider it, and it influences you. That snake could not hurt them. Why? Because it was made of brass. It had been rendered powerless. If only those who have been bitten by sin would look upon Calvary and consider that sin has been rendered powerless! If only those who have been bitten by sickness would look and see that the judgment of God has rendered sickness powerless!

We need to look upon it and see that all the sin and the sickness of an entire world came upon Jesus Christ because He *became sin*. In doing so, He *became sick* and bore all sicknesses, all diseases, and every infirmity known to mankind.

In Psalm 22, David had a revelation of the events that would take place in the future when Jesus would hang on the tree, or cross:

My God, my God why hast thou forsaken me? why art thou so far from helping me, and from the words of my roaring?

Jesus repeated those very words when He was crucified at Calvary:

> **I am poured out like water, all my bones are out of joint: my heart is like wax; it is melted in the midst of my bowels.**
>
> **My strength is dried up like a potsherd; and my tongue cleaveth to my jaws; and thou hast brought me into the dust of death.**
>
> **For dogs have compassed me: the assembly of the wicked have inclosed me: they pierced my hands and my feet.**
>
> **I may tell all my bones: they look and stare upon me.**
>
> **They part my garments among them, and cast lots upon my vesture.**
>
> **Psalm 22:14-18**

This psalm is prophetic, speaking of Jesus Christ as He was crucified. As we read it, we realize that the curse of mankind came upon Jesus in that hour. Only a man under a curse would speak those words. We deserved this judgment; we earned it. But Jesus came and took the curse for us. He suffered so we do not need to.

Don't ever say, "I am going to suffer like Jesus. I want to be just like Jesus and suffer." *Jesus suffered so you do not need to!* You do not need to take that curse on you. If you do, it isn't going to do any good for anybody else.

Don't ever pray, "God, do not let my husband (wife, etc.) die; take my life instead. God, if You have to make me sick to heal them, then do it." *Don't ever pray that!* Jesus has already taken the curse for them. You do not have to, and you can't! When you pray such a prayer, you are opening yourself up for the devil to attack you. *He* is the one who steals, kills, and destroys, according to John 10:10.

Jesus was the only one who was *worthy*; the only one who was *holy*; the only one who was *sinless*; and it was *only His blood that could bring salvation. Only His body could bring healing.* As He was placed upon that tree, or cross, His body was broken, and He was ravaged with sickness and disease. That curse overcame Him.

As I was studying, I found this quotation: "A curse that has overtaken its victim is a spent force." *Jesus Christ Himself took the full force of the curse and it ended there at Calvary.* The curse has no right — it has no power — because Jesus Christ redeemed us from the curse of the law according to Galatians 3:13. *The curse has already been reversed!*

Decide To Believe

How do we receive healing? It takes our decision to believe that the curse of sickness has already been reversed. It takes our decision to believe, regardless of the circumstances. It takes our decision to believe God's Word above *everything*. It doesn't matter who lives, dies, gets sick, or gets healed; we must believe the Word *regardless* of what happens in this world. We must believe that the curse was reversed, and that Jesus Christ Himself bore sickness, pain, and every infirmity. We must believe it regardless of what happens to any person, because it is the Word of God — and it is forever established in the heavens.

Pray this prayer with me now:

Father God, I believe that your Word is true, and it is forever established in the heavens. I believe that Jesus Christ took away my sickness and my disease by the stripes on His back. Christ has redeemed me from the curse of sickness; therefore, healing is His will for me. I am free from the curse of sickness and disease!

Chapter 12
Activate God's Power in Your Body

Since you have established in your mind that the curse of sickness has been reversed by Jesus Christ, your heart is now open to receive His healing power!

Let's look at the vital side, the experiential side, the reality, of receiving the healing power of God into your body. Healing is already established. It's done. That's a legal fact. But there is a difference between that fact and the fact that there are still people who have not received their healing.

Let's look in the Word of God and find out how this healing power is administered to the body so that divine health can become a reality.

> And a certain woman, which had an issue of blood twelve years,
>
> And had suffered many things of many physicians, and had spent all

> **that she had, and was nothing bettered, but rather grew worse,**
>
> **When she had heard of Jesus, came in the press behind, and touched his garment.**
>
> **For she said, if I may touch but his clothes, I shall be whole.**
>
> Mark 5:25-28

Regardless of what people are saying about confession and the power of the spoken Word, confession is a principle seen throughout the entire Bible. This woman *said* and *spoke* her faith. She did not say, "If I can touch His garment, maybe I can get something." No. She said, "If I may touch but His clothes, I *shall* be whole." That was her faith speaking.

Speak and Act Your Faith

In order to activate God's power in our bodies and in our lives, we must *speak* our faith and *act* our faith.

One of the biggest lies that the devil has ever perpetrated upon the Body of Christ is, "If we *believe* in healing, we will be all right."

It is not enough just to believe in healing. There are thousands of people who die every day who believe in healing! They believe in the miraculous healing power of

God. But the devil has caused them to substitute *belief* for *action*.

I was raised in a church that believed in divine healing. It was one of the doctrines of our denomination. When we joined the church, we signed a little card that *said* we believed in healing. The pastor believed in healing. When that denomination began, it was established upon the belief of the healing power of God and miracles. The reason they had to separate from other churches was because they believed in healing. But in the 18 years that I attended that church, I cannot remember one person being healed there! Isn't that astounding? To attend a church that would fight over the fact that they believed in divine healing, yet not see anyone receive healing is a shame.

The Touch of Faith

There is a difference between *believing* in healing and *appropriating* that healing for your own body. Don't let the devil put you in a state of apathy because you *believe* in healing. Healing is something we must reach out in faith to obtain for ourselves.

So this woman said, *"If I may touch but his clothes, I shall be whole."* We see faith speaking here. *"And straightway the fountain of her blood was dried up; and she felt in her body that she was healed of that plague."* She touched Jesus!

> And Jesus, immediately knowing in himself that virtue had gone out of him, turned him about in the press, and said, Who touched my clothes?
>
> And his disciples said unto him, **Thou seest the multitude thronging thee, and sayest thou, Who touched me?**
>
> And he looked round about to see her that had done this thing.
>
> But the woman fearing and trembling, knowing what was done in her, came and fell down before him, and told him all the truth.
>
> And he said unto her, Daughter, thy faith hath made thee whole; go in peace, and be whole of thy plague.
>
> **Mark 5:30-34**

These people had all heard about Jesus' healing power and those who had been delivered and set free. They crowded around, pushing, shoving, and touching Him. As Jesus was being pushed along by the crowd, He said, "Who touched Me?"

His disciples were amazed and said, "What do You mean, who touched You? Everyone is touching You!"

Many people today are crying out for healing, filling auditoriums, seeking the healing power of God. But *it is the touch of faith that activates the power of God!* The difference between that woman and those who just pressed around Jesus was this: She *said*, "I shall be whole," and her *touch* was the touch of faith.

Faith is what draws upon that healing power. This is the difference. This woman had heard the good report. Someone told her about healing and Jesus' ministry. She chose to believe. Then she activated God's power by reaching out in faith and touching Jesus.

You may believe in healing, but in order to receive it into your body, that power must be activated by faith. But how do you do it?

You begin to say this right now: "I will receive the healing power into my body." Say it now! "I will receive the healing power into my body."

Now think about that for just a moment. You have made your decision, just as this woman in the Bible made her decision.

The Healing Force of God

An interesting point in verse thirty is that Jesus knew in Himself that virtue had gone out of Him. What does that mean? Most people do not really know what that "virtue" is. It is *power*.

What we are studying here is a tangible anointing of the Spirit of God. The virtue that flowed out of Jesus is a tangible force. It is a reality. It can be felt. It is not mind over matter, Christian Science, or spiritualism. It is a force that is a heavenly materiality. It is a force that heals and sets free.

> **And it shall come to pass in that day, that his burden shall be taken away from off thy shoulder, and his yoke from off thy neck, and the yoke shall be destroyed because of the anointing.**
>
> **Isaiah 10:27**

This force is from God, and it was manifested because of Jesus Christ. Healing power is like the electricity in a room: It is dormant until someone goes over and flips the light switch, and then it flows and the lights come on. The force of electricity is in the walls of a room, hidden in the wires. It is unseen, but if you stick your finger into an electric outlet, you'll find out that it is there! Similiarly, the healing power of God, the virtue of Christ, is a tangible substance. When activated it is unseen but present. It can actually be *felt*.

When I encountered the Charismatic Movement in the early 1970s, the thing that caught my attention was the fact they believed that you could be healed *now.* You could have a miracle *now.* Not only did they believe it; it happened!

As I began to travel and teach in these circles, the Spirit of God spoke to me and told me, "I have placed the healing power of God upon you, and as you go forth and lay hands upon people, that power will flow out of you into them, and you will see healings and miracles." I did not feel anything when He said that to me, but the very next time someone asked me to pray for them, as I laid my hands upon them, I felt something rush out of me into them, and they were instantly healed by the power of God.

As I continued to minister along those lines, I occasionally saw people who would have a gradual healing — they would improve with each day. Some healings were instantaneous, but some were gradual. But I would always know when that healing virtue would flow out of me. I would also know when it would *not* flow out of me. It is not something special that I have. It is the healing power of God. I have chosen to yield myself to Him; therefore, it flows through me.

85

I was in a meeting in South Texas when a group of people came forward to be prayed for. As I began to minister to them, the healing power of God went into them. However, as I laid my hands upon a certain woman, the healing power of God would not go into her. I thought it was strange, but I continued to pray for the others, and I left her alone. I found out later that this woman was a witch who came to disrupt the meetings.

When I lay hands upon people, the power of God will go into them, but if they try to receive it in the mental realm, it will come back out. The power is not received by your *mind*, but by your *spirit*. When I lay hands on people, I usually tell them not to try to receive it with their mind, but to relax and allow that power to flow throughout their body. The woman with the issue of blood did not receive healing through an exercise of her mind, but through an exercise of her faith — and faith is born of the spirit.

A Point of Contact To Release Faith

Another way in which we can receive the healing power of God is by touching:

And he came down with them,

and stood in the plain, and the company of his disciples, and a great multitude of people out of all Judaea and Jerusalem, and from the sea coast of Tyre and Sidon, which came to hear him, and to be healed of their diseases;

And they that were vexed with unclean spirits: and they were healed.

And the whole multitude sought to touch him: for there went virtue out of him, and healed them all.

Luke 6:17-19

Notice that the whole multitude sought to touch Him, for there went virtue — or power — out of Him. By touching, you can release your faith for healing. One woman was healed when a healing evangelist on the radio told his audience to touch the radio as a point of contact to release their faith. The radio had no healing power, but the faith the people released at that point brought healing. Also, through the laying on of hands, the power of God can be transmitted, as I'm sure it was with the multitude surrounding Jesus.

Helping Others To Receive

And it came to pass on a certain day, As he was teaching, that there were Pharisees and doctors of the law

> sitting by, which were come out of
> every town of Galilee, and Judaea,
> and Jerusalem: and the power of the
> Lord was present to heal them.
>
> **Luke 5:17**

The power of the Lord that was present
was strong enough to heal every person in
that place! Continuing to read the rest of the
chapter, we find that *not one other person in the
house was healed that day!* Isn't that sad?
. . . *"The power of the Lord was present to heal
them,"* the Bible says, yet only one man in
the whole crowd *received* that power.

> And, behold, men brought in a
> bed a man which was taken with a
> palsy: and they sought means to
> bring him in, and to lay him before
> him.
>
> And when they could not find by
> what way they might bring him in
> because of the multitude, they went
> upon the housetop and let him down
> through the tiling with his couch into
> the midst before Jesus.
>
> And when he saw their faith, he
> said unto him, Man, thy sins are for-
> given thee.
>
> **Luke 5:18-20**

I want you to notice something else here.
It says, "When He saw *their* faith." Jesus

took notice of the combined faith that was present in the man's friends. This should be an encouragement to those of you who are believing for healing for someone else.

There is a time when people are not able to exercise faith on their own behalf. We as the Body of Christ need to stand together and exercise our faith to draw upon the healing power of God for others. It is all too easy to say, "Well, they did not get healed because they didn't have faith."

There is power in agreement. We need to lay hold of the healing power of God for each other. There are times when other people just aren't able to receive it for themselves, and we need to take some of that responsibility ourselves.

Ultimately, however, it is left up to the individual who is sick. Their will is involved. If they do not *want* to live, and they *refuse* to believe, then it is their choice. But there are others who *want* to be healed, but they need a little help from us. That is where we can come into agreement and see their healing manifest.

This man so greatly desired to be healed that he allowed his friends to lower him through the roof of a house. That took faith! His faith was rewarded when Jesus said,

"Arise, and take up thy couch, and go into thine house." The man obeyed Jesus' command, *"and departed to his own house, glorifying God."*

Chapter 13
Why Do Healing Evangelists Become Ill?

Tremendous miracles have taken place through the ministries of the great healing evangelists of our time. In some cases, people who did not even believe in God or miracles would walk into a miracle service conducted by one of these healing evangelists and receive an instantaneous healing.

People have stumbled over the fact that the so-called "healing minister" later became ill or died. They say, "I don't understand this. If the power of God came into operation and all those people were healed, why did the evangelist get sick? Why did he or she die?"

The reason is because healings that take place in meetings like that are a special manifestation of the Holy Spirit. This is different from using your own faith like the woman with the issue of blood did. She went to

Jesus *expecting* to receive, because she had *heard* the Word.

The gifts of healings operate most of the time in the presence of unbelievers, as a sign and a wonder to them. These healings are like a dinner bell to bring the unsaved to Christ. And many unsaved have come to meetings, received miraculous healings, and then received Jesus as their Savior.

The evangelist who is being used by God in the gifts of healings is still required to use his own faith in the Word of God to receive divine health and divine healing for his own body. Why? Because the gifts of healings are not manifested for the benefit of the individual who is ministering. They are for the benefit of the people.

Never stumble over what happened to someone else. Never forsake the Word of God because of what happened to someone else. The Word of God is true, regardless of what happens to others.

Elisha had the healing power of God in his life, as we see from the miracles that took place in his ministry. There was so much power left in his *bones* that after he was dead, some men threw a corpse into Elisha's grave, and the dead man was resurrected (2 Kings 13:21).

On the other hand, the power of God can be present to heal but still not be received by the person in need. Happily, this did not happen in a meeting I once held in South Texas. As I started to speak, I saw a woman sitting on the front row with the presence of God all over her. I became so intrigued that I walked over and said, "Excuse me, but do you need healing or something?" She began to cry, and she said, "I've already received it. This warmth just came all over me. I had an asthma attack and could not breathe. I was going to leave the meeting, but now I can breathe!" We all worshipped and praised God. Then I went back to my text.

When I looked up again, I saw the same thing happen with a man on the back row. I stared at him for a moment. (By this time I was beginning to catch on.) I said, "Excuse me, sir — back there in the back — you with the brown coat on. Do you need healing or something?"

He said, "I was healed right before you spoke to me. I had surgery on my back, and I have not been able to move. Now I feel fine." He began to move around, and he demonstrated his healing.

We rejoiced and praised God, and again I went back to my Scripture. I never did get to read that Scripture, because each time I looked up, I would see the Spirit of God moving on someone else. That night there were many people who instantly received a miraculous manifestation of healing in their body. This was a different manifestation of the gifts of healing in operation. Some did not expect to be healed. Others did, but God's power was there to heal *everyone*.

In the early years of my ministry as I prayed for people, the anointing would flow from my hands and go into their body. But God is not limited to the use of hands. Once as I was ministering in Dallas, I felt that power move from my hands to my mouth. I sensed that the anointing was in my mouth, and now I was to *speak* forth the healings. So I immediately stopped laying hands on people and started to speak forth the healings that I knew were taking place.

It is so important to flow with that anointing. At times I still lay hands on people. At other times I speak forth the healings. I have even been in meetings where there was total silence for thirty minutes or an hour, and people were healed during the silence.

The Holy Spirit knows the perfect order for every service. We need to follow Him.

Over the years I have seen various manifestations of the gifts of healings in my own ministry, but I have always had to use my own faith in God's Word for my healing. There have been times that I have been attacked with illness in my body, but as I ministered, many were healed, even though I did not feel well. I had to receive *my* healing through faith and acting on God's Word.

Chapter 14
Healing Through the Spoken Word

In Matthew 8 we read the story of a Roman centurion.

> And when Jesus was entered into Capernaum, there came unto him a centurion, beseeching him,
>
> And saying, Lord, my servant lieth at home sick of the palsy, grievously tormented.
>
> And Jesus saith unto him, I will come and heal him.
>
> Matthew 8:5-7

Jesus Was Willing To Make a Personal Appearance

What a cause for rejoicing! The man did not know if Jesus would come or not, but Jesus said, "I will come to your house, and I will heal him." How many of us would have jumped up and down rejoicing because Jesus was coming to our house! To this man, however, a personal visit was not necessary.

> **The centurion answered and said, Lord, I am not worthy that thou shouldest come under my roof: but speak the word only, and my servant shall be healed.**

> **For I am a man under authority, having soldiers under me: and I say to this man, Go, and he goeth; and to another, Come, and he cometh; and to my servant, Do this, and he doeth it.**

> **When Jesus heard it, he marvelled, and said to them that followed, Verily I say unto you, I have not found so great faith, no, not in Israel.**

> **Matthew 8:8-10**

Jesus had just told this man that He would make a personal appearance to heal the servant. The man replied, "No, do not do that. You do not have to. I know what authority is, for I am a man who has some authority. I have servants, and I say, 'Go,' and they go. I recognize that You are a man of authority, and You do not even need to come to my house. All you have to do is *speak* the Word, and the authority of your Word will give my servant perfect healing." And Jesus marveled at his faith!

What happened? Jesus said to the centurion, *"Go thy way; and as thou hast believed, so be it done unto thee. And his servant was healed in the selfsame hour"* (Matt. 8:13).

Healing Through a Word of Knowledge in Denver

The centurion received the miracle for his servant by accepting Jesus' spoken word. You, too, can receive the healing anointing of God through the spoken word. Perhaps the word you receive will be a gift of the word of knowledge given in a meeting where God's power is manifest.

I was in Denver for a meeting when I sensed the power of God moving, and I began to speak forth the healings. A woman in that service had a problem with her neck. As the word was spoken forth, she felt the warmth of the healing power of God go over her neck, and it was released. She came to the front to give her testimony, so I walked up to her with the microphone. She fell under the power of God.

When she got up, I went back to her, and she fell over again. Finally, we just went ahead with the meeting. The next day she gave her testimony. She had been healed in her neck, and she had not even thought to ask God to heal her leg. She was born with the tibia bone in one leg shorter than the other one. Consequently, she wore a built-up heel on one shoe. When she came forward to give her testimony about the healing in her neck, she did not think to ask for healing for her leg. All she knew was every time I walked past her, she fell down.

She went home that night, got in the bathtub, looked down, and saw that her knees were even for the first time in her life. She said, "I am going to have to believe God for the money to buy new shoes, because I cannot walk in these things now." She was healed of her neck ailment by a spoken word, and then God performed a creative miracle in her legs!

Chapter 15
You Don't Have To Wait

God does not have you on a waiting list. He wants you well — *now*!

He was teaching in one of the synagogues on the sabbath.

And, behold, there was a woman which had a spirit of infirmity eighteen years, and was bowed together, and could in no wise lift up herself.

Luke 13:10,11

What a terrible state to be in! Did you know that some diseases, sicknesses, and infirmities are caused by evil spirits? They have to be cast out of the body. That does not mean that the person is demon possessed; it means there is a spirit that has oppressed their body, and it has to be dealt with.

And when Jesus saw her, he called her to him, and said unto her, Woman, thou art loosed from thine infirmity.

Luke 13:12

What a strange thing to say. Here is a

101

woman, bent over, who cannot even straighten herself up, and this man tells her she is free from her problem!

I'm sure she thought, "How can you say I am loosed from my infirmity when I am bent over and cannot even straighten up?" Jesus called things that were not as though they were: *"Woman, thou art loosed from thine infirmity."*

The woman was still bent over. She had no physical evidence of her freedom, but Jesus said she was free! He first spoke the Word to her. She did not straighten up, so He laid His hands on her. Isn't it wonderful that Jesus did *not* turn and say to her, "Because you didn't receive healing through my spoken Word, you are going to have to stay sick."

I want you to know that God wants you well any way He can get you well. If you cannot receive healing through the spoken Word, He will try to get you to receive through the laying on of hands. If you cannot receive through the laying on of hands, you can call for the elders of the church. If you cannot receive healing through the elders of the church, there are doctors who can help you until you can receive your healing. But *God wants you well any way He can get you there.*

God has not demanded that we receive our healing in only one manner. He has given us many ways in which we can receive. So when this woman could not receive her healing from the spoken Word, Jesus laid His hands upon her, *". . . and immediately she was made straight, and glorified God"* (Luke 13:13).

Have you ever noticed that when people are made well and whole, they never glorify the devil? Don't tell me that healing is from the devil, because everyone I have seen healed in a healing service glorified God. Wouldn't you think if a member of your congregation had been bent over for eighteen years and was suddenly made well that everyone would be excited and praise God over this wonderful miracle? Not in this synagogue.

Miracles Stir Religious Jealousy

And the ruler of the synagogue answered with indignation. . . .

Luke 13:14

I don't know why it says he *answered*, because nobody *asked* him anything. He was angry. Why? *". . . Because that Jesus had healed on the sabbath day. . . ."* Of all things, Jesus the Son of God did not know that you are not supposed to do good works and heal people on the Sabbath! It was thought to be a sin.

Isn't it funny how people get so wrapped up in tradition? There was a woman in my hometown who was a Christian and belonged to a certain church. This woman was so sick, she had almost every conceivable thing wrong with her. In fact, every time she went to the doctor she was told that she might fall dead anytime.

One night she and her husband heard a knock on their door. A couple came in and said, "We were having Bible study tonight, and we felt like we should come and pray for you. Do you mind?"

She said, "No, go ahead. Go right ahead."

They joined hands and began to pray. As they prayed, the power of God went through the sick woman, and she was instantly healed of every condition in her body. She and her husband went back to their church to tell everybody, "You don't have to bring food anymore. You do not have to help us financially anymore. You don't have to do anything. I've been healed by the power of God!"

They said, "Well, you can come to

church, but just do not tell anybody you have been healed." They reversed the blessing of God into a curse. Now that she is healed, they act as though she has a curse.

This is how the people in this synagogue behaved when the woman was loosed from her infirmity. "My goodness, Jesus — don't You know You aren't supposed to do this on the sabbath day?" The ruler said, *"There are six days in which men ought to work: in them therefore come and be healed, and not on the sabbath day. The Lord then answered him, and said, Thou hypocrite, doth not each one of you on the sabbath loose his ox or his ass from the stall, and lead him away to watering?"* (Luke 13:14,15).

God Wants You Well Now!

And ought not this woman, being a daughter of Abraham, whom Satan hath bound, lo, these eighteen years, be loosed from this bond on the sabbath day?

Luke 13:16

Notice it did not say *God* had bound her. Jesus was saying that this woman who is a daughter of Abraham should not have to bear this disease one more day. She should not have to wait until the next morning to be healed.

And you do not have to wait until tomorrow to be healed. You, too, are children of Abraham, heirs of the promise, and you have no need to wait one more day with sickness or infirmity in your body.

You do not have to wait to be loosed from any bondage — emotional, mental, or physical. You can receive your healing *now!* You can be loosed from every chain *now!*

Pray this prayer with me now:

> *Lord Jesus, I receive your healing power into my body now to drive out every sickness, disease, and infirmity. I receive healing in my body now through the power of Jesus' Name!*

For a complete catalog of CDs, DVDs, and books by Annette Capps write:
Annette Capps Ministries
PO Box 10
Broken Arrow, OK 74013
Or call
1-877-396-9400

Visit our online bookstore at:
www.annettecapps.com